Leonard Trask, the Wonderful Invalid

Written by Leonard Trask
Restoration and Forward
by Wesley Clayton

For more information on Ankylosing Spondylitis, visit
EverydayBattle.com

Forward
by Wesley Clayton

When I was first diagnosed with ankylosing spondylitis, I felt like I'd received a death sentence.

Ankylosing spondylitis is a form of arthritis that mostly impacts the spine, but additional painful symptoms are common: swollen joints, inflammation of the internal organs and eyeballs, and gradual fusion of the vertebrae that can leave the sufferer painfully stiff at best and completely immobilized at worst.

I'd been suffering from all the classic symptoms (and then some) for about two years before I stumbled across a rheumatologist who was able to decipher my illness for me - also notifying me that this fresh diagnosis was completely incurable.

Luckily for me, 'incurable' doesn't translate to 'untreatable.' Through the miracle of modern medicine, we've been able to develop new treatments that can help slow the disease for many patients. Furthermore, research has been accelerating in recent decades that sheds light on certain lifestyle changes that can help minimize symptoms. Low impact exercise, diet, and mental wellness have all shown promising results for the modern ankylosing spondylitis patient.

Despite this progress, it takes an average of seven years to diagnose ankylosing spondylitis - making my excruciating two year wait look like only a brief layover on the way to treatment.

My initial research into this disease that I could barely spell, let alone pronounce, lead to me the text you are now reading from: _A Brief Historical Sketch of the Life and Sufferings of Leonard Trask: The Wonderful Invalid._

Originally published around 1860, this autobiographical account details the life of a man living in Maine at the time. It follows Leonard Trask's gradual descent into the infirmity of a disease that, at the time, had no name and no treatment. It documents his entire life, from start to near-finish, including his hopes and fears. More importantly, it documents his sense of humor, his optimism, and his determination to live life to its fullest.

Leonard Trask lived during a time when selling oneself as a 'medical curiosity' to the public was not an uncommon practice. Despite his attempts to make his living as a farmer, the progressive disease eventually took its toll and Trask, struggling to provide for his family, wrote and sold this autobiography to the public.

Within a year or two of it's publication, Leonard Trask was laid to rest in Peru, Maine, but his story has continued to impact future generations. In 2003, the American College of Rheumatology recognized his book as 'the first clinical description in the American literature of a patient with ankylosing spondylitis.'

For those of you keeping count: it took Trask a full 170 years to get his ankylosing spondylitis diagnosis - dwarfing even the average wait by more than a century and a half!

By republishing this, it's my hope that Leonard Trask's story is one that comforts other ankylosing spondylitis sufferers and their friends and families, too. Trask lived not only without treatment options, but a diagnosis wasn't even possible. Yet, through his writings I was able to find a hope and resilience that I believe other ankylosing spondylitis patients can benefit from.

I've worked hard to maintain the original spirit of this story. In transcribing Trask's words, I have limited my textual edits mostly to structural elements and had all the original artwork digitally enhanced without any direct changes made to them. Otherwise, you will find everything exactly as Trask originally published it.

Like Trask, himself, I've found a great deal of relief in being able to share my own ankylosing spondylitis story. If you're looking for more information related to ankylosing spondylitis, it's sources, it's treatments, and more, please feel free to read my story at http://www.everydaybattle.com.

Wesley Clayton

wes@everydaybattle.com

Introduction.

It is the opinion of many, that a certain fatality attends the life and actions of people, whereby the strange events of their lives are shaped, and to which, their success or defeat, their good or bad luck, their misfortunes or prosperity, are attributed. In the brief sketch which follows, it is not the object to prove or disprove the correctness or fallacy of this idea, but to exemplify how mysteriously the hand of Providence sometimes preserves the creature, man, when accident overtakes him, while at other times, a seeming trifle - the smallest mishaps, prove fatal, and happiness - all the enjoyments of life - and even life itself, are eventually destroyed, if not extinguished, in a moment.

Great and disastrous consequences are sometimes the result of seemingly small causes - while light catastrophes are the result of causes, appearing at first momentous, the anticipated, horrid consequences of which, might seem unavoidable. In the short story of Mr. Trask, it will be seen that he has had many hair-breadth escapes for life, and has been for many years the unlucky and afflicted child of sickness, disappointment, and misfortune.

He now appears among his fellow citizens, a walking wonder - a living evidence of what his system has undergone, and the bodily sufferings and pain he has endured - while his case presents to the astonished eye, a marvelous picture finding, probably, no parallel in the arena of humanity.

Yet the wonder is not, that he has met with many accidents, and endured much pain; but that after all which he has endured, he still survives; and, in full possession of his mental faculties, reasons, reflects, loves, hates and hopes like other men, and clings to life and life's enjoyments, with all the tenacity of his earlier years, breasting the torrent of life's ills and troubles, with the determined resolution and "iron will" of former and brighter days.

He was once an athletic and muscular man - symmetrical in person - broad chest and shoulders - erect in form, and stately in his movements, presenting to the eye a picture of health and strength. That symmetry has now departed, those once powerful muscles have become feeble - that agile step falters - and a mere wreck is all that remains of the physical man!

His extraordinary sufferings - his accidental deformity - his rigid spine, and bowed head - the result of injury and disease - furnish a striking proof of the physical powers of the man, and of the capacity of the human frame to endure rack, contortions and contractions, and still the vital spark remain unextinguished. Wherever he appears, among strangers, he excites their wonder and astonishment; and curiosity leads them to ask him many questions, which common civility, and the kindness and sympathy manifested by inquirers, prompt him to answer.

Such interrogatories as the following are with him frequent occurrences: "How came you in this condition?" "Were you born so?" "Are you a native of this country?" "How long have you been in this way?": "Have you tried to get help?" - "What did physicians do for you?" "Do you suffer any pain?" To give a full verbal history of his accidents, his treatment, and all matters connected therewith, to every friendly inquirer, was tiresome if not entirely impracticable. This led him to the conclusion, that a concise history of the whole transactions, connected with his present deformity, might be useful and interesting to the public, especially so to those whom he should meet, and who, in person, should witness his singular misfortune.

High-minded and influential men, from various localities, who have seen him laboring with his hands for the small income of a few pence per day, to sustain himself and family in an independent position, have told him, that many men were before the public, making fortunes out of persons and things less wonderful than he, and which excited less the curiosity of people than he - that as he had been by accident deprived of the power to labor with profit to himself, like other men - and was, probably, the most singular case known in the Union, if not on the whole globe - he ought to avail himself of the means misfortune had left him to procure a competence, to make himself and feeble dependents comfortable. That if he would exhibit himself before his fellow-men, he would be sure to accomplish his wishes, and obtain that pecuniary relief so desirable. But family and home were dear to him, and while he possessed the power to labor, although for small pay, and at the expense of bodily ease and comfort, he chose to depend on the labor of his own hands for a livelihood, rather than on the wonder, sympathy or curiosity of the community.

Disease continuing its ravages upon his system, he soon found himself unable to perform his accustomed labor, and concluded to publish this little work, hoping for the sale of the same - which he intends to conduct in person - to realize a sufficient remuneration to sustain himself and such dependents as now looked to him for support and protection.

It is not for the morsel that may satiate the cravings of to-day, for which he would exercise and devote his remaining energies, while the morrow frowns with the prospect of destitution and want; neither is it for garments to clothe the shivering limbs for the moment, while advancing winter scowls with threatening storms of tempest and snow - but he seeks from the sale of his little book, or some other laudable course, to obtain the means of better enjoying life in some suitable avocation or position, better adapted to the exercise of the remaining faculties and powers of his body and mind. With this frank and open exposition of his wishes, purpose and motive, he throws himself upon the kind indulgence of a generous community, whose patronage he has received encouragement to expect.

In presenting his brief history to the public, he has made no attempt at high-colored flourishing, exaggeration or fiction - deeming it unnecessary to resort to fanciful embellishments, or enter the broad field of fiction, when truth - as in this case - rides above the giddy flights of imagination. He has endeavored to make his story as short and as interesting as a plain statement of facts would justify; and he now offers it to a generous and candid public, with full confidence that it will meet with a kind reception at the hands of his more fortunate fellow-citizens - whose liberal patronage he respectfully solicits, and whos favors will command his gratitude and thanks.

THE AUTHOR.
L. TRASK

'Leonard Trask, in 1833.'

LEONARD TRASK: THE WONDERFUL INVALID.

Mr. Leonard Trask - the subject of the following historical sketch - was born in the town of Hartford, in the County of Oxford, and State of Maine, June 30, 1805. His parents were respectable and industrious people. His father - Mr. Osborne Trask, was the son of Mr. Samuel Trask - a native of Sutton - now Millbury - in Worcester County, and State of Massachusetts.

He resided in what was formerly called the North Parish, in that part of the town familiarly termed Grassy Hill, and moved to the District of Maine awhile before the birth of Leonard. He was the son of Mr. Samuel Trask, whose offspring - the fruits of three marriages - numbered twenty-one - his first, second and third wife, each bearing him seven children. From this progeny, the Trask family has become somewhat numerous and widely scattered, mostly over the New England States.

Mr. Osborne Trask was one of the pioneers who settled in the town of Hartford, where he reared a family of children. He was diligent and enterprising, and soon attained to prosperous circumstances, and a comfortable degree of wealth and independence. Being an industrious and economical farmer, he early taught his children the necessity and benefit of useful toil, prudence and perseverance.

The years of Leonard's minority were massed like the early years of most of the dutiful sons of farmers, in assisting his father in the labors of the farm. He was faithful to the interests of his father; served and obeyed him with the true respect and fidelity of a good son, until he was twenty-one years of age, and became a man for himself.

With this brief notice of the minor, we pass to that period of his life when, as his own man, and free from parental control, he began to manage for himself, and labor for his own interest and emolument. The first labor which he performed after he became free, was done in the town of Carthage, where he worked at making bricks, at eleven and a half dollars per month. In the autumn of 1826, having completed the term for which he engaged in the brick-yard, he returned to Hartford, and took a job to build 100 rods of wall, for $100. He bought a pair of oxen, for which he paid $50, and went to work with them on his job of building wall.

He labored almost incessantly, day and night, and completed his job in eight weeks. He then sold his oxen for $55, taking an obligation for neat stock, to be paid whenever he should want it. He then went into the lumber, or "logging swamp," in the town of Byron, and labored two and half months at twelve dollars per month.

Having finished his labor in the swamp, he left the woods on Saturday, and the next Monday morning shouldered his pack, and wended his way on foot towards Massachusetts, whither many young men resorted, to seek employment and money. He found employment in the town of Millbury, the place of his father's nativity, and labored for Mr. Aaron Trask, his uncle, during the first year, at thirteen dollars per month.

The next year, he labored on the farm of Mr. Jonathan Trask, on Grassy Hill, at eighteen dollars per month.

Having thus obtained a small sum, which he wished to invest in land, for a future farm, he returned to Maine, and purchased some wild land in the new and sparsely settled town of Peru. He next contracted for a barn to be built on his newly purchased land, for which he gave his next year's labor.

The next year, being the twenty-sixth year of his life, he spent in building a house on his land, working with unremitting diligence by day, and much in the night, sleeping but a small portion of his time, until his house was completed and ready to receive its tenants.

Being of a hardy and almost iron constitution, he performed labor and endured hardships that would have shattered and broken down the constitution and health of most men. The same year he married with Eunice Knight, a worthy and interesting daughter of Mr. G. Knight, a prosperous and wealthy farmer in Peru, his adopted town. Though somewhat younger than himself, she had been educated in all the duties of housewifery, and proved herself a fit mate for the industrious and persevering young farmer.

Thus, in his twenty-seventh year, Mr. T. commenced house-keeping, with lively hopes of future prosperity. With the labor of his own hands, he had accumulated the means of starting fair in life, and, as he supposed, had laid the foundation of future competence and success. From the proceeds of the oxen, which he had previously sold, and a small surplus of his wages, not invested in land, he was enabled to stock his farm with one pair of oxen, two cows, two yearlings, six sheep, and one yearling colt.

For a while success attended him in all his undertakings. His wild land began to assume the appearance of a well cultivated farm. Rich fields of grain, hay and corn now flourished in place of the forest and brushwood, which his diligent hands had removed. HIs barn was filled with hay; his chamber with grain and the golden ears of corn. "Children were born to him," and he and his worthy and industrious bride rejoiced in the pleasing prospect of rearing their tender babes with their own hands, in affluence and plenty, unseared and unmolested by that poverty and pinching want that often embitters the life of the indigent, the wretched, and the suffering poor.

Little thought that hale and happy couple, while caressing their little ones, and rejoicing over their well-deserved prosperity, that ere ten years should roll away, misfortune, sorrow and destitution, should creep in at their door - that health, and the prospect of earthly enjoyment, should have fled their dwelling, to be their guests no more.

Little thought they, that ere ten years should pass away, their early hopes and promising prospects should be forever blighted, and hopeless misery should sit, the ruling queen at their once happy fireside - that these lent blessings of heaven, these tender offsprings, on whom they doted, should be compelled by the stern mandates of fate, to share with them the ills, afflictions, and deprivations incident to dire misfortune. Little thought they that in less than ten years, that robust and athletic form should become bowed - that broad, expanded chest contracted, and the once erect and powerful man, a mere wreck of what he once had been. But such was the fate which Dame Fortune, while she smiled on the morning of his life, had reserved for his future years. Such is often the result of aspiring hopes, and early and visionary dreams of future happiness and success.

About the year 1833, while Mr. T. was riding on horseback through a neighboring town, a "luckless hog," in the highway, hearing the approach of a horseman, took fright, and as is often the case with that perverse animal, to flee from danger took the opposite direction from a place of safety, and rushed directly under the horse's feet. The frightened horse, as a matter of course, stumbled and plunged, throwing his rider directly over his head. Mr. T. was thrown with great force upon the ground.

Receiving the full force of the fall upon the neck and shoulders. This gave so severe a shock to the spinal column, that he was unable to reach his home for several days.

'Artists rendition of the pig tripping the horse, rider falling head-first to the ground'

Two months or more elapsed before he was able to do any kind of labor. He then attempted to do some light work, but it was performed with extreme difficulty and pain. During the rest of that season, he performed a portion of the farm work, laboring while he was unable to endure toil more than an hour at a time, sitting down in the fields at intervals to rest, while the pain in the spine, at the suspension of toil, would partially abate. Wearily he dragged out the residue of that season.

The next year he enjoyed better health. He could work with more ease, and continue longer at toil, without experiencing very severe pain; and he began to entertain hopes that he should perfectly recover, and again attain to his former vigor and activity.

He was still young, and the fire and mettle of former years had not entirely departed. He was desirous of worldly gain; and zeal and ambition to see his farm flourish, and wealthy increase, led him to tax his physical powers beyond what a strict regard for health, or the sound judgment and discretion of mature years might have dictated.

During that year, as though fate had determined to add affliction to affliction, and heap misfortune upon misfortune, he sustained severe losses in property, and discouraging reverse of his former prosperity.

"His cattle died, and blighted was his corn."

He owned at the time eighteen head of neat cattle, one horse and twenty sheep. That fatal disease among cattle, known as "bloody murrain," began to prevail among his stock. He lost by it, nine cows, four oxen, and several smaller cattle. His horse also sickened and died. Subsequently he lost three other horses.

These losses and sudden reverse of fortune, weighed heavily upon the unfortunate man, and the pinching want of money led him, as of yore, to seek it in the timber swamp of Maine. In the winter season, he hired out to labor in the Dead River "Pineries." When he first went into the woods, the snow was four feet deep. The location of the lumbering operations was twelve miles from any dwelling. The camp, which the lumbering party expected to find, had been destroyed and they found themselves at night in the woods without shelter, and unable to construct one for the first night. Consequently they spent a severe winter night in the open air, leaning against, or traveling around the trees.

The next day was spent in wallowing about, seeking for, and determining upon a location for a camp. The second night was passed like the first, around their fire in the open air. The next day they constructed a camp; and the third night they slept soundly on cold hemlock boughs, above the snowy, frozen and damp ground. In consequence of this exposure, Mr. T. took a severe cold, and his spinal difficulty revived with increasing torture. He supposed it to be an attack of rheumatism, and strove to drive it off by exercise.

Such was the lameness in his back and neck, that while going to and from camp, he was unable to keep up with the other hands; and it was not till he had exercised some time, and got warmed up, that he could perform any labor, without suffering the most excruciating pain. He affirms, that while performing his daily and customary labor, and all that could be expected from any hand, he had often been forced to take his food in his hands, and eat it while traveling around a stump, the pain in his neck being so severe that he could not endure it and eat.

He was unable to rise from his couch of straw and boughs, without the assistance of a rope with which to draw himself up. Still he performed his daily task with the rest of the lumbermen, through the winter, which to him was long and tedious.

In the spring following, his increasing infirmity and severe pain admonished him of the serious nature of his disease. The neck and spine between the scapulars, or shoulder bones, began to curve, and he began to bow forward, growing, as we usually term it, "round shouldered." He employed the medical service of Dr. Chaplin, of Dixfield, but experienced no benefit therefrom.

He next applied to Dr. Stanley, of the same town. The remedy resorted to was cupping, and a seton in the back of the neck. This proved ineffectual also. Dr. Farwell, then of Dixfield, was next consulted. He prescribed a lobelia emetic, together with some other mild treatment. This availed nothing, the patient still growing worse. The advice and medical treatment of Dr. G. W. Turner, of Dixfield, a skillful and popular physician, was next sought. Besides giving medicine internally, Dr. T. ordered blisters upon the back of the neck, and also made deep incisions, or cuts with the knife, up and down, on each side of the spine.

This treatment, although torturing, was borne with patience by the suffering man, together with the excruciating pains of the disease, which was bowing him down and drawing the spine into a circular form. The next physician consulted was Dr. C. Holland, of Canton, a celebrated physician of extensive practice and popularity.

His treatment was much the same as those who had preceded him. He resorted to blistering and cupping; put a seton in the patient's neck, and occasionally gave an emetic. His success was no better than that of others in removing the disease; the patient continuing to suffer the torments of medical treatment, adding to the miseries of an almost insufferable disease.

Mr. T. next sought relief by calling to his aid the skillful service of Dr. B. K. Swasey, of Canton. But the baffled physician retired from the field, with no better success than those who had preceded him. The medical skill of Dr. Banks, of Canton, was also called into requisition. He made the experiment of bleeding the patient. After exhausting the system by drawing a large portion of blood from the patient's veins, Dr. B. left him in such a prostrate condition that several months elapsed before he was restored to that degree of strength which he enjoyed before he received the treatment.

In the summer after this year, it began about the year 1840, he fell from a load of hay while riding from the field whither he had been to oversee some of the work of the farm. The injury occasioned by the fall, brought on a fever which prostrated him for several months. He was attended by Dr. B. Carey, of Sumner. He finally recovered of the fever; but the disease of the spine grew worse.

At this period there appeared to be, or in fact there was, a parting of the vertebrae of the neck and back, or upper part of the spine. This was attended with a noise like the low crack of a whip, or of the finger joints, which was distinctly heard by such persons as chanced to be present.

When this separation of the joints occurred, the invalid experienced a shock and fell prostrated to the ground, or floor, and was unable to rise, or even move for one or two hours, and sometimes longer.

This was attributed by some physicians to the escape of synovia, or joint water. Most likely the shock upon the nervous system was occasioned by the sudden derangement of the column of nerves, or spinal column, to which the nerves all tend. At this stage of the disease, the head became dizzy, and a partial blindness of the eyes ensued. The top of the head, over the cerebrum, or upper brain, became numb.

Medical assistance was sought from Dr. Leach, of Canton. Supposing the difficulty to be caused by a rush of blood to the head, Dr. L. resorted to bleeding. This only reduced the patient and made him worse.

Being tired of enduring the treatment of physicians of the "regular practice," which was only adding pain and torture to the suffering he already endured, without the least prospect of benefit resulting therefrom, Mr. T. had recourse to Dr. J. W. Smith, alias J. W. Kittridge, of the Thomsonian mode of practice. Having treated the patient liberally with a bed full of boiled potatoes, jugs of hot water, and bountiful potations of gin and lobelia, Dr. S. retired from the contest in despair, leaving the suffering man to vomit up his dizzy head and spinal complaint as best he could.

It was near this period that the wife of Mr. T., worn down with the care and fatigue attending upon her sick husband, fell sick, and was attacked with hemorrhage or bleeding at the lungs. She was for some time under the care of a physician, and has continued in feeble and delicate health up to the present time.

The next physician employed by Mr. T. was Dr. Drake, who was also of the Thompsonian practice. In his treatment, a tub of cold water was ordered, and a liberal pile of stones was heated. The patient was placed over the tub and a coverlet or quilt thrown over him, the hot stones were then carefully moved back and forth from the fire to the tub, and from the tub to the fire, till the patient was in a high state of perspiration. He was then placed in a bed, and lobelia freely administered. On his last visit when the patient had attained to a desirable state of "vomitation," Dr. D. left to attend to other duties.

As ill luck would have it, when the sick man had vomited to his heart's content the inexorable lobelia would give him no respite, nor cease its demands upon his heaving stomach. When he had continued to vomit for twelve hours his attendant became alarmed, and resorted to "pig-weed tea," to counteract the influence of the stubborn lobelia. This soon restored quiet to the stomach, and the invalid came out of the contest, receiving no benefit, except the pleasure of vomiting twelve hours or more, and a full knowledge of the powerful agency of lobelia in expelling substances from the stomach. From this time his patronage of the Thompsonians was not very extensive.

In the autumn of 1841, he was again attached with a fever which had a long run. He was attended by Drs. Carey of Sumner, and Bridgham of Buckfield. From the year 1841 to 1843 he continued seeking relief from the chronic disease with which he was continually suffering, by consulting and following the prescriptions of the best physicians he could find.

Twenty-two physicians were employed at different periods, among whom not mentioned were Drs. Coolidge and the younger Bridgham of Buckfield, Snow of LIvermore, Bragg of Hartford, Comstock of Sumner, &c., &c. Dr A. K. Kittridge of Paris, usually accounted the surgeon in Oxford County, being usually resorted to in critical and severe cases of disease of the bones or muscles, was consulted, and relief sought to be obtained from his experienced hand. After a careful examination, Dr. K. told the patient plainly, that his case was hopeless. He advised him to spend no more money for medicine or medical aid, telling him that he might follow prescriptions till the last remnant of his property was exhausted, but no benefit would be likely to result therefrom.

It is said, "While there is life there still is hope." It was hard for Mr. Trask to yield to the stern necessity of his fate while any proposed remedy affording the least encouragement to hope had not been tried and exhausted. Chancing one day in 1843 to pick up a hand bill or advertisement of Dr. S. C. Hewitt of Boston, a gleam of hope once more entered his mind and he determined to make one more effort for the recovery of health, or at least to obtain partial relief from pain, and, if possible, a suspension or stay of his increasing deformity.

Gathering a small sum from the remnant of his property, he went to Boston, there to make the last struggle with a grim disease that was making his days and nights tedious and gloomy, and reducing him in stature and increasing his deformity. He tarried with Dr. H. three weeks, enduring the hot water treatment and the attempts made to strengthen him by mechanical force till his waning strength failed, and his system could endure no more.

His physician declared his condition hopeless, and advised him to return to his friends. Then the last ray of hope of better days fled forever from his heart. He returned to his home in Maine, penniless and desponding, to drag out his wearisome and painful life with his tender wife and dependent children, in distressing labor, disappointment, perplexity, and want.

From the year 1843 up to the present period (1858), his life has been a continued series of afflictions, privations, and pain. Fever after fever has followed him. Physicians' bills have been multiplied and extended. From the time he returned from Boston, his neck and back have continued to curve more and more, every year drawing his head downward upon his breast, till there appears but little room to press it farther, without stopping entirely the movement of his jaws.

The rounding of the shoulders has deranged the clavicles, or collar bones, pressing the sternum, or breastbone, upon the lungs, and contracting the cavity of the chest. This, in the fall of 1845, produced a violent cough which followed him through the whole of the next year. His physician pronounced his case consumption, and gave him up to die. But his constitution, which had so long resisted disease, once more came off victor, and he survived. The lungs obtained space for action, and though in an unnatural position, they still performed their usual functions.

His lungs have never attained to a healthy state, and a slight cough usually attends him. Palpitation of the heart, heat and pain in the top of the head, and in the neck, are difficulties daily experienced. Notwithstanding his infirmities, Mr. T. has always continued to labor for a livelihood and sustenance for himself and family.

Many kinds of farming work he has been totally unable to perform, yet a few kinds he has managed to perform tolerably well. For many years he could hoe very well, working in inverse order, backward instead of forward. Framing business being so hard for him, and the small amount he could perform being of so little importance and income, he has frequently resorted to peddling small articles of traffic.

His success in this pursuit, while he was able to perform it, was defeated by his uncouth figure and deformity. The ladies and children were frequently frightened and fled whenever he made a call. This was an unfortunate state of things for a peddler whose manner of deal brought him into social communion with the "fair sex," and to mingle often in the society of women and children.

As an illustration of this inconvenience, Mr. T. relates an incident. Being out on a peddling excursion, he had traveled some distance without coming to a dwelling, and grew apprehensive that he had missed his way. Before him at a distance, he saw a house. With the intention of inquiring his way, and selling some of his wares, he directed his course towards it.

Before reaching it, he saw a lady leave the house and run into a thicket of weeds and bushes not far distant, and hide herself. Being desirous of learning his own latitude and longitude, he waited and watched intently the weeds for her appearance. Soon he saw a head peep up from among the weeds; but as he remained before the door, it soon popped down again. He continued waiting for some time. While he continued waiting, the head continued popping, until, tired of waiting for the return of the fugitive, and supposing himself to be the cause, he departed, traveling two or three miles off his way.

He next came to a house and rapped at the door. No one appeared to be within. He opened the door, being weary and faint, deliberately walked in and took a seat. No one was there. Finding a newspaper on the table, he took it and began to peruse it. The inmates of the house, having great confidence in the "reading portion of the community," soon began to make their appearance from different parts of the house, concluding that anything that could read, very likely was human.

Mr. T. continued to peddle at times until his neck became so stiff, and his head so bowed down, that straining his eyes in looking up to guide his horse, caused the blood frequently to run from them down his cheeks. His wife asserts that though she had seen him while enduring far more severe suffering, yet to see the blood trickle from his eyes down his face, was the most distressing sight she had ever witnessed.

In 1853, Mr. T. was thrown from his wagon, breaking four of his ribs, and injuring or breaking one of the collar bones. For many years he has felt unsafe when riding alone, being in continual danger of accidents on account of his inability to discover objects any distance before him. Traveling on foot, when he was able to do it, was attended with like liability to accident, not only to himself but to others. One or two incidents among the many, will serve to illustrate the disadvantages he labored under, in traveling in the road, even from neighbor to neighbor.

Having occasion, on a certain time, to go a short distance from home, he was walking very slowly, as he was always under the necessity of doing, when he heard a noise and sudden crash ahead. Being unable to see but a few feet before him without bending backwards, he halted to see what was the cause. A few rods in front, he saw a horse and carriage. The horse was attempting to "right about face," to "beat a retreat," while a gentleman and lady, the occupants of the carriage, were in the act of alighting upon a hedge fence by the road side, whither they had been thrown by the sudden upsetting of the carriage, occasioned by the abrupt retreat of the horse.

To go to their relief would only make the matter worse. He therefore remained quiet, waiting the result. When the horse had been quieted and pacified, the lady rescued and the carriage righted, the exasperated gentleman, with the whip uplifted, advanced upon the innocent cripple - "You damn nuisance," said he, "why are you here frightening my horse? I will teach you better manners! I will flog you out of your skin!"

'The horse, on seeing Mr. Trask, became frightened.'

The cripple, being unable to retreat, plead innocent, and asked pardon for the offense. On learning the state of the case, and finding it was not a trick played to frighten the horse, the gentleman's wrath abated, and he concluded to let the invalid off without a thrashing. He retired, saying, that "Such a man had no right to appear in the streets; but if he must go out, the community ought to furnish him with a horse and carriage."

At another time, while passing a short distance in the road, he met a gentleman alone in a carriage, whose horse took fright, became unmanageable, and cleared himself from the wagon; and it was not until the horse was blinded that he would allow the unfortunate man to pass. The gentleman sustained the accident very quietly saying to the cripple, "Your misfortune is greater than mine."

Thus, in the autumn of life, Mr. T. finds himself cut off by disease and misfortune, from those modes of gaining his livelihood common to his fellow men. The peculiarity of his disease and form prevents him from exercising the powers and faculties of body and mind which are still left him, in sustaining a feeble wife and three children of slender constitutions, which he might exercise were his infirmities of an ordinary character.

Amidst all his misfortunes, Mr. T. has succeeded in sustaining his family up to the present date. His children, seven in all, (some of whom have arrived to majority, and others have married and left him), have always been privileged to associate in the family circle around the parental hearth, sustained and protected by a father's hand.

Though starting in life with ardent hopes of prosperity, and having exerted all his powers to stem the torrent of earthly ills with which he has been visited, he finds himself in the decline of life bowed down with disease, as we see him in the picture, the "child of sorrow" and the deformed victim of sickness and pain.

He has no power to move his head up or down, to the right or left, without moving his whole body; his neck, and upper part of the back, having become perfectly rigid, and the whole upper part of the spinal column, in the opinion of skillful physicians, has become ossified.

On account of his strange and peculiar form, many showmen have attempted to hire him in order to take him before the public for exhibition. His reply has ever been, that his misfortunes and afflictions, his pains and sufferings, were his own; his singular figure and deformity were his own, - and as it had pleased God so to afflict him, that he had become a living, human curiosity, and a wonder to his fellow men, he would sell or hire himself to no man, to become a source of speculation in their hands - that though in his physical appearance he scarcely bore the resemblance of humanity, yet through the benignity of kind Providence, the "man within" had been left unimpaired; and if his singular form presented to the mind of his fellow men a subject of curiosity, wonder, interest, or instruction, the sight should become a source of profit to no one but himself.

Many who may have seen him in years past, bowed down, yet toiling with his hands from morning till night for the small income of a few pence per day, have advised him "to throw himself upon the town," telling him that such a man ought not to labor, and that such pauperism could not be considered a disgrace to him. But his soul revolted at the thought.

He had a wife, the idol of his heart's first affections, whose protector and supporter he had promised to be, in the heyday of his prosperity and manly pride. It was she, who, like a guardian angel, had watched by his bedside through his protracted sickness, till her health, too, was gone.

Could he see her at each annual circuit of the sun placed upon the "pauper block," that anti-Christian mart for "human chattels," and struck off to the lowest bidder at public outcry? Could he lay aside his rights as a free and independent citizen, and lose his identity and the control of himself, and place himself beside his tender companion and be sold with her at public auction, like cattle in the shambles? Could he see his little children, feeble and helpless, who clung like tendrils round his heart, virtually become fatherless and motherless, and dragged from his control and from the kind care of a loving mother, separated from each other, and sold, or bound out he not whither? No! he could not endure this!

He could see the remnant of his hard earnings vanish from him and find its way into the pockets of physicians who had done him no good, or otherwise expended for the wants of himself and family - he could endure privation and poverty, he could endure pain even to the rending asunder of bone from bone in his mortal frame - he could endure all this; yet he could not endure that the only earthly treasure which his heart valued, and all that cruel fate and misfortune had left to him should be torn from the care of their parents and consigned to the care of strangers and forever inherit the name of paupers!

Consequently the energies of the whole man, mind and body, were employed to sustain himself and family; and thus far he has been successful.

In his prime, he was erect, of symmetrical proportion, - standing six feet one inch in his boots, and weighing 199 pounds. To his chin he now measures three feet nine and a half inches; and to his shoulders, which are now the summit of the trunk, he measures four feet ten and a half inches, and weighs about 134 pounds.

It is hoped that the perusal of this short sketch of the life of one whose form presents a picture to the eye rarely met in the arena of humanity, may admonish us of the transitory nature of sublunary hopes and prospects - the delusive and fleeting character of earthly bliss; that it may teach the young the priceless value of health - the greatest earthly blessing which heaven bestows on man; that while they enjoy it, they may not be careless in its protections, nor barter it for worldly gain; that it may admonish them how soon may be the transit from joy to sorrow, from hope to despair; and from the height of worldly pleasure to the depth of human woe; that it may school the hearts of all while in prosperity and health to a due appreciation of the blessings they enjoy; that while they behold the unfortunate condition of their fellow-men and consider how much happier and more fortunate has been their lot,

"The conscious heart of charity may warm," and they may be led to seek that true felicity, that Heaven born happiness that flows from a consciousness of making others happy around them.

ANECDOTES OF MR. TRASK.

It has often been the misfortune of Mr. Trask to experience in person the effect of the Lever Power when it has attained the advantage and an unintended control over him. A few interesting incidents, fresh in his recollections, he will relate.

When about nineteen years of age, while laboring for his father, he was engaged one day with three other hands, among whom was his elder brother, in what the pioneers of Maine usually call "junking" - which means cutting up timber into convenient junks for piling. It was sometimes the case, that at the outskirts of the woods, and sometimes deeper in the forest, large trees were turned up by the roots, taking with them some extent of the surface of the ground - such part, for instance, as adhered to the roots.

The soil upon the roots of a large tree, such as the towering hemlock, formed a heavy weight, continually urging the tree to an upright position. It was frequently the practice of those who first cleared the wild lands, especially for pasturage, to cut the trees off at some distance from the root, as thereby they saved the labor of cutting through the burly part of the tree nearer the roots.

In the course of the day before mentioned, the gang of choppers had occasion to junk a large hemlock of the description just named. The tree had a heavy root, and laid across another which was near the butt, elevating the trunk and top gradually some distance from the ground.

The dexterity of the axemen had been frequently tried during the day, by seeing who would "butt" the others, all working on the same tree. If the man nearest the roots could succeed in cutting the tree off quicker than those above him, he claimed it as a victory - he had "butted" his companions.

Leonard being ambitious of excelling whenever he had a competitor, undertook the butt cut of this tree. The idea that his companions were some distance from the ground, and if he could succeed in "dropping" them, he should gain some fun from the operation, in addition to his claim of superiority, nerved him to a full display of his axemanship. Each exerted himself to his full power.

Leonard gained the victory, but in the end found himself, like Haman, "caught in his own toil." In order to succeed, he had left a longer stump than usual, and when it was nearly off, he stepped entirely on it to avoid going down with the other, or top part of the tree. The timber began to crack, giving notice that the top part was about to fall. "Halloo there at the top," said Leonard, "take care of your trotters!" and gave one more blow, not suspecting it would finish the work. But while lifting his axe for another blow, the trap sprung - the tree dropped in an instant - the loaded roots fell back to their original place, raising the stump to a perpendicular, with a sweep and velocity that sent the unlucky operator flying in the air.

He reached the ground some twelve or fifteen feet from the stump, the edge of his axe, in its fall, barely grazing his head. He escaped with bones unbroken, but badly bruised, and had the mortification of finding the laugh turned on himself instead of his companions, they having retreated in season to avoid the fall.

TRASK AND ELDER.

At a certain time during the winter in which Mr. Trask worked in the swamp on Dead River, after his unfortunate fall from his horse, he was engaged with several other hands, among whom was a Mr. Elder, in getting from the forest a very large and long pine log. It was so situated that they were under the necessity of hauling it top foremost.

The road was upon a side hill, and the heavy butt end manifested a strong inclination to roll downhill upon the lower side of the road. Coming to a place where the road pitched over the brow of a small rise or hill, the top or foremost end of the log, together with the sled, became elevated, the heavy rear end keeping close to the ground.

This gave the timber a fair opportunity to roll downhill, sled and all, the sled to which the log was bound being no impediment when it was raised clear of the ground. Mr. Trask, seeing the state of things, determined to counteract the force of gravity by resorting to the power of the lever. Seizing a lever and passing it under the log and rave of the sled, and over the hither rave, he threw his weight upon it, determining to keep the sled right side up; Mr. Elder came to his assistance, grasped the end of the lever and held it down.

As the team advanced, higher rose the end of the log and sled, and higher, still higher, were Trask and Elder elevated in the air. The courage of Elder soon began to wane, and he manifested a disposition to get his feet on terra firma. "Hold on, Elder," said Mr. T., "she is almost on a poise; we will soon break her down." But higher rose the top of the massive pine, and higher rose the sled, lever and weights; till Mr. Elder, either fearing to go higher, or wishing to "spit upon his hands to take a better hold," slipped from the lever, leaving Mr. T. alone suspended on it.

The weight of the two was barely sufficient to prevent the log from rolling, and on losing part of the impediment, it immediately rolled, giving an impetus and velocity to the lever which sent Mr. T. against a tree on the opposite side of the road, many feet from the ground. He was thrown with such celerity and force, and the collision was so violent, that his first thought on falling to the ground was, that "he was no better than a dead man." But finding himself much better than dead, he soon began to reflect on the conduct of the recreant partner, who had deserted him in the hour of danger, and at the critical moment, when desertion without notice was sure to be followed by disaster - risky, if not fatal.

MR. TRASK IN PURSUIT OF FUEL.

'Trask balanced on a felled tree, like a seesaw.'

A few years ago, some time after Mr. T.'s neck became perfectly stiff, he got out of fuel. It was in the winter season, and the snow deep. He took his axe and went into the woods alone to procure some. He chopped off a small sized tree, and in falling it lodged upon another tree. He stepped a few feet in the opposite direction from the way the tree had begun to fall, and leaned backward, as is his custom when he wishes to look up, to see what prevented the tree from falling. It was cut completely off; and while he was prepared to look, it started, the butt slipping till it placed him astride of it.

The top then came down, performing a complete maneuver of the lever power - the tree being the lever, the stump the fulcrum, and Mr. T. the weight to be raised. Mr. T. was not aware of the operation until he found himself six or eight feet in the air and about to alight on the other side of the stump. He came out of the affair badly bruised, and not very well satisfied with this exhibition of the lever power.

MR. TRASK AT THE CIRCUS.

A few years since, Sand's Circus visited the little village of D. Such an exhibition being a rare occurrence in the place, Mr. and Mrs. Trask took it into their minds to attend. Mrs. Trask took the tickets and passed them to the door-keeper. They were both passing in among the crowd when the keeper cried out "Halloo there, old fellow, you need not think to sneak by me in that way, creeping under the ladies' shawls," and he seized the cripple by the collar and dragged him back.

"Ah!" said Mr. T., "it is sometimes a pleasure and sometimes a misfortune to have one's head drawn towards the ladies. It is not because my head is down here that I would complain, but because I cannot get it up."

The keeper discovered his mistake, asked pardon for his rashness, and the cripple passed on.

MR. TRASK GOING TO DRINK.

Through the village of C. runs a small mill-stream, which is filled to the banks by dams crossing below. Two bridges cross the stream but a short distance from each other, and the ground between is trodden to the water's edge, resembling the highway. Mr. T. was once in the village on business, and having occasion to cross one of the bridges, missed the direction and walked directly into the stream between the bridges. A friend discovering him in the act of stepping in, called out, "Where are you going?" "Going to drink," said Mr. T.; "but the dish is a little too large for convenience."

'Leonard Trask, from a daguerreotype taken in 1857.'

TO MY PATRONS.

Ye favored thousands of our happy land,
Who, blest with health, with peace and competence,
Before your fellow hale, erect can stand,
Enjoying all the sweets of every sense;

While your fair brows, you heavenward raise with ease,
Beholding all the bustlin scenes around,
And me, unshapely, bow'd with dire disease,
My vision stinted, all my frame unsound;

With thankfulness, with gratitude and praise
To Him, whose watchful eye is over all,
Your hearts, your minds, your voice to Heaven raise,
That my misfortune did not you befall.

And while your limbs are hale and free from pain,
Health blooming, your companion, night and day,
At poverty repine not, nor complain,
Though gold and riches lie not in your way.

Would you, who thirst for wealth and power desire,
When you my uncouth form and sufferings see,
Your longing wish to gratify, retire
From the hale circle, and exchange with me?

Would all the gold which California yields,
Tempt you to take my form, and aching head?
Or all the wealth that's reaped on India's fields?
If not, reflect how sad my lot, indeed!

Would you whose coffers gold and silver fill,
Whose income yearly, hundred thousands tell,
Choose rather, if the choice were at your will,
Become like me, or all your wealth expel?

If you all wealth would banish from your sight -
Would health and form preserve whate'er they cost;
By this criterion, exercised aright,
You may appreciate what I have lost.

I would not, friends, excite your mirth or glee,
Nor down your cheek induce the tears to roll,
Unless those tears again could gathered be,
To the calm fountain of the tranquil soul;

And there excite the peaceful, quiet mind
To resignation, placid, sweet content,
And gratitude to heaven, good and kind,
Who, to your lot, has better fortune sent.

Yet, think not, while affliction's cruel hand
Presses me down, and holds unyielding sway,
That I, a human, living wonder stand,
Stoic in soul, with heart as cold as clay.

With joy I often look to Heaven above,
Thank God for mercies and benignant care,
Rejoice, that through his kind and tender love,
I still so many earthly blessings share.

I thank him that the hearts of men are kind,
That while I live and wander here below,

So many sympathizing friend I find,
Such friendly treatment, too, where'er I go.

I'm thankful, too, that woman's angel heart,
The same in every clime, in every land,
In sorrow's vestry, always acts its part,
To raise the abject with tender hand.

Though gay and sportive, as fairy queen,
How soon she melts at scenes of bitter woe!
Down her fairy cheeks, my eyes have often seen,
The crystal fountain of her heart to flow.

I've seen her in the village - in the town -
In crowded streets, and marked the silent tear;
I've met her sig, but ne'er her haughty frown -
Her words unpleasant never greet my ear.

In towns and cities, little children kind,
Treat not the cripple scornfully nor rude;

Among them many precious friend I find,
With minds and hearts like little angels good.
They look with wonder, pity and surprise,
Nor insult, to my sorrows, ever add;
From them no shouts of ridicule arise;
Their kindness, too, has oft my heart made glad.

Through many a seeming long and tedious year,
Such torture racked my mortal, shattered frame,
That grateful, thankful - ever joy sincere
I feel, at relaxation of my pain.

In resignation there is joy and peace,
Whate'er my lot, whate'er my form may be;
Faith, Hope and Charity, those joys increase,
And soothe my mind in dark adversity.

In that celestial, bright and happy land,
Beyond this vale of sorrow, pain and tears,
Where I, erect in glory, hope to stand,
In faith and hope, the future bright appears.

I thank you kindly, sympathizing friends -
Your favors, your kind patronage implore;
On these alone my earthly weal depends -
Farewell - and peace be with you evermore.

L. TRASK.

APPENDIX.

On the 24th of May, 1858, Mr. L. Trask, the unfortunate subject of the preceding pages, received an injury, if not surpassing, certainly equal to any accident of his eventful life. Early on the morning of that day he left his home in Peru, accompanied by his wife, and, together with several other passengers, took the stagecoach, designing to go to Strickland's Ferry, in Livermore.

The coach was heavily loaded with passengers and baggage, - the inside being filled to repletion, while several were under the necessity of taking a "deck passage," and were seated on the top of the vehicle. All went on without any mishap as far as Britton's Mills, in Livermore. The driver reined up his horses in front of the post office in that village, stopping a few minutes for the purpose of changing the mail.

The post office being located a few rods off the direct line of travel to the Ferry, the carriage had to return a short distance on the same road it came. Although the ground was very smooth and level in front of the office, and the room for turning ample for any team, yet, by the carelessness and haste of the drive in making the turn, the coach was suddenly upset, when the passengers and baggage were hurled in one promiscuous heap to the ground.

There were few among them who escaped without some injury; but none were so seriously hurt as Mr. T. Sitting on the opposite side of the carriage from the way it fell, he was first elevated, and then pitched head first against the other side of the coach, which was then on the ground. Being unable to get hold of anything to break the force of the fall, his head came in contact with a projecting iron in the door of the coach, which parted the scalp, opening a gash in his head five inches long, and penetrating to the skull bone.

By the aid of the bystanders the coach was soon righted, and the passengers taken out. Mr. T., bleeding and almost lifeless, was carried to the house of Dr. Barnard, which fortunately was nearby. Dr. B., after sewing up and dressing the wound in the head, found that his most serious injury was in his neck, jaws and chest.

By the violence of the fall, the chin and jaws were driven further down upon the bones below as to stop the circulation in the flesh between them, which afterwards came out to the bones by putrefaction. Of his head Mr. T. made no complaint, but suffered intolerably with pain in the jaws and neck. Scarcely any one, except himself, thought he would ever recover or even survive but a short time.

His physician notified him in the afternoon of the day of the accident, that he would probably not survive till the next morning. He replied that he thought he should soon be able to return home. Several days after this, a certain skillful and experienced physician, and an old acquaintance and friend of Mr. T., told him he could never recover, and must soon die. He very promptly replied, "I shall get about again; my time has not come yet," - and so it proved.

The chin and jaws continued for many days to press still harder upon the chest, increasing irritation and inflammation, and no means could for a long time be devised to relieve him, or keep the head from pressing down more and more each day.

At length, an experiment, made by Dr. Bartlett of Dixfield succeeded. Dr. Bartlett put a pad on the forehead, and a bandage around the head. Through this he passed a small cord, doubled it, and made it fast to the wall of the room by means of a staple at the head of the patient's bed. By twisting the cord with a small rod, the head could be drawn back or let down at the pleasure of the operator. In this situation, Mr. T. lay day and night, from the first of June till the last of August. By keeping the chin from pressing upon the chest, air was admitted between them, and his wounds finally healed.

After suffering for three months, he was able to walk again, with no other alteration in his appearance, except that his head is now drawn down about an inch or inch and a half lower than it was before the stage-coach accident.

Printed in Great Britain
by Amazon